PROMPTS & QUESTIONS
TO DEEPEN YOUR KNOWLEDGE

365 Days
to Know Yourself

JOURNAL

365 Days to Know Yourself Journal

2023 YGTMedia Co. Press Trade Paperback Edition.

Copyright © 2023 Brittany Bird

Published in Canada,
for Global Distribution by YGTMedia Co.

www.ygtmedia.co

For more information email: publishing@ygtmedia.co

ISBN trade paperback: 978-1-998754-43-4

To order additional copies of this book:
publishing@ygtmedia.co

365 Days
to Know Yourself

BRITTANY A. BIRD

HOW TO USE THIS JOURNAL:

The intention behind the *365 Days to Know Yourself Journal* is to encourage you to really turn inward. You will get out of it what you put in. Some of the questions may trigger you, and that's okay. To be honest, it's part of my goal. I just ask you to be aware of when it happens, then get curious as to why. Change happens when we are able to get uncomfortable and be honest with ourselves.

It can be exciting to get a new journal, and you may feel you really want to do more than just one prompt; however, it's recommended that you only do one to two entries per day to allow the question(s) to sit with you so you can reflect.

If you think the question is easy, I ask you to look deeper.

You may notice that throughout the journal there are a couple of "similar" questions. This is intentional. They are not the same. The questions are asked in different ways to prompt a different perspective; they are also asked at different stages of the self-development you are gaining through this work.

My ask is that you don't limit yourself to the lines provided for each prompt. Everyone is different, so grab an extra notebook if you need it. This is your journey and reflection, so only you will know when the prompt is complete.

I hope you enjoy these questions as much as I did and that you find you know yourself a little more each day.

P.S. Some of these prompts can be asked daily, monthly, and yearly to really ensure you are being true to yourself and are in alignment with what works for *you*.

Who are you?

What do you need today? This week? This month?

How do you connect with yourself?

What makes you tick?

(What gets you excited? What makes you feel happy and at ease?)

What do you unconditionally love about yourself?

What would it take
to believe in yourself?

What does happiness
mean to you?

Does your definition of happiness rely
on something that may happen in the future?
If so, would you declare that happiness?

What is the truth behind the stories you are telling yourself?

(Everyone tells themselves stories. Some are positive, some are negative. Some hold us back and some push us forward, but these are the stories that "limit" us from accomplishing what it is we need/want.)

9

What is the truth behind the emotions you're feeling?

(Ask yourself: Are they mine? Do they belong to me? Am I feeling sadness, anger, rage, or is it something more deeply rooted underneath that?)

What are your values and morals?

(If it helps, holistic lifestyle coach Paul Chek defines core values as codes of conduct we live by that entail morals and ethics. Morals represent those codes that are life-affirmative.)

What are your values and morals around your health, happiness, self-care, relationships, etc.?

Are your behaviors in alignment with your values in each category?

Are your behaviors in alignment
with your morals in each category?

Which people in your life are unaligned with
your values and morals? Do these people influence
you from following your values and morals?

_____

_____

_____

_____

_____

_____

_____

_____

_____

_____

What shared value(s) do you hold with your friends, family, and all relationships that are most dear to you?

Who are the people you can call upon for support?

Who are the people
that will celebrate your success?

17

In looking at the last two questions, are the people you can call and the people who celebrate your success the same? Who just shows up for the celebration, and why do you think that is?

What is your dream? Do the decisions/choices
you make bring you closer to your dreams?
Which ones do you feel are impeding them?
Which ones are moving you toward your dreams?

Your consciousness mirrors your health
and your health mirrors your consciousness.
How healthy would you say each are?

Our bodies are always communicating with us.
Are you listening? Listen to your body. Feel it.
What message does it have for you?

(To listen to your body, close your eyes and take a deep breath. Where do you feel tension / heaviness / any unwanted feeling or any feeling other than peace/calmness? Take note of that. Now ask what it is. Allow yourself to listen wholeheartedly with curiosity.)

That feeling that you can't shake sometimes:
feel into it. Does it all belong to you? Does part of it
belong to you? Does none of it belong to you?

When did you stop looking at the world
with curious eyes? Why do you think that is?

When you stop being curious, you stop loving
in a sense. What are you curious about?

If you want to know what belief systems you have, listen to your language. What words actively come out of your mouth? About yourself, about life, about others? What meaning do these words hold? Reflect on the language. Is it more negative than positive?

Are you making decisions based on instant gratification? Reflect on your daily decisions, big and small. What percent of decisions are made for instant gratification?

What do you want to change in your life?

Are you willing to change for something?
What means enough for you to change?

What if there was no wrong choice,
how would your world change?

Are you filling your own cup?

(Are you taking time to fill your needs on the regular?)

Do you truly trust yourself?
Why or why not?

31

What would happen if you actually listened
to yourself and your body?

What if all the answers you seek are inside you?
How would that change things for you?

33

With everything you've learned so far,
what would you want to say to your younger self?
The self that had the hardest time?

Are you living through your own or someone
else's ideas instead of being in the present?

What if I told you happiness favors us all?
What would that shift for you?
What would you do differently in knowing that?

_____

_____

_____

_____

_____

_____

_____

_____

_____

If you released the judgment you have for yourself,
how would your life change?

37

What are your external
(or extrinsic) goals?

What are your internal
(or intrinsic) goals?

What do YOU really want in this moment?
In one year? In five years? In ten years?

What do you wish to learn
in this lifetime?

If you looked at the word "no" as
Next Opportunity, what would that do for you?

It's the simple things in life that you do consistently
that will help you grow the most. So, what are you
doing consistently? Which things do you need
to stop and which do you need to continue?
What do you need to start doing consistently
so you can arrive at where you want to be?

You deserve to have your own life;
do you believe that? Are all your wants and needs
truly your own? Which ones are yours
and which ones belong to someone else?

_____

_____

_____

_____

_____

_____

_____

_____

_____

_____

If I told you that you can have access to the world
to relay one message, what would it be right now?

Believing is where your thinking stops,
so where does your personal thinking start?

Our free will is something that can only be made
when we consciously make the choice
to do something. Are you using your own
free will to reject being healthy or happy?

Emotions are just energy in motion.
When we are stuck on an emotion, it's just energy
that has become stagnant. So, what energy
have you been stuck on lately?

Your shadow self is as full of light *(potential)* as it is dark *(limitations)*. "Shadow" is a term defined by Carl Jung as "the dark unlit part of the ego." The ego is what we know about consciously and what we are. The shadow is the part we fail to usually see and know. If you were to truly look within, what have you been failing / not wanting to see within yourself?

We sometimes project our ego in one way,
as a hero, so someone else has to carry
that heaviness/responsibility for us.
Who is playing the hero in your life?

Many of us are in a constant state of wanting
to fix something in ourselves or others.
If you look at your current life and relationship
with yourself and others, what are you trying to fix?

*(If you harmonize the yin and yang within,
you'll realize that things do not need to be fixed.)*

Behaviors are addictive. Which behaviors
have you been / are you addicted to?

What would it be like if you released
the judgment you hold for others?

Which negative thoughts, emotions,
and behaviors that you are holding on to
are weighing you down? Which aren't serving you?
Which positive ones have been lifting you up
and serving you? Are they still serving you?

(These things are always changing, so it's always great to review them.)

Is there a memory or experience with a friend/boss/ parent/sibling/stranger that you can't let go of? Consider their external influences as to why they may have done something. You may know what it was, or you may not know exactly. I challenge you to consider it *(this doesn't mean you have to agree with it; however, empathy is key here)*. When you do consider their external influences, how do your body and emotions change when you think of this experience/ memory?

(You'll shift from judgment to a curious state.)

What does acceptance mean to you?

What would it look like
to accept yourself?

What resistance do you have inside yourself?

The mind will only believe something based on
what it's been taught / what it's been through,
seen, read, etc. Our body gives unbiased feedback.
Gut feelings are based on the body, not the mind.
Reflect on what you rely on more, the body
or the mind. Do you feel it needs to change?

If you could change one of your behaviors,
what would it be? Why?

Where do you believe you learned the behavior you wish to change?

(You have the ability to change your behavior, but you must first understand it.)

How has this behavior served you and/or
the person you learned it from in the past?

What makes you excited
to get out of bed in the morning?

What personality trait
do you love about yourself and why?

Are you taking care of your body or just ensuring it runs? List everything you do to take care of your body and connect with each thing. Are you doing each thing because you know the body enjoys it, or is it something you are just doing because you "should"?

Remember:
Food is more than just energy. It is information.
What information are you giving to yourself?
Does your body need/want that information?

You are allowed to say "no" for yourself.
What would you like to say no to?

Power comes from within. Looking outward
only creates/allows for a false image.
Where are you creating a false image in your life?

All the pain, emotion, and stress you are feeling
have a reason to them. It's okay to feel them. Now,
you need to understand them and be willing to change
them. Are you willing to sit with them and listen
so you can change? If so, start with just sitting with
them. Where are they sitting in the body?
Where do you feel the heaviness?

*(Do this with each feeling and see if the place
in your body differs with each one.)*

Go back to each pain/emotion/stress from the previous question and focus on the heaviness of one of those stressors at a time. Sit with it and just observe. Is it a color? Is it a shape? Is it constantly changing?

*(Keep sitting with it and just allow it to be.
What does the emotion/heaviness feel like once you are done?)*

When we look to receive external gratification for reassurance, we have instantly lost our inner motivator. When a person doesn't reassure us, it can be devastating. What are you truly seeking when looking for external gratification?

How easy is it for you to give?
What do you feel when you give?

How easy is it for you to receive?
What do you feel when you receive?

(Take note on whether giving or receiving is easier/harder and why.)

Be honest with yourself:
What are your insecurities?

Where/when did these insecurities develop? When reflecting on them, do the memories you hold have as much value/hurt as they did when they happened?

Whatever "triggers" you most usually has the biggest lesson. What is/are your biggest trigger(s)?

Life can only let you down as much as you let it.
How much are you allowing it to let you down?

People can only let you down as much as you
let them. Who are you allowing to let you down?

You can grow your inner strength just by believing you can. How are you going to start believing you can?

Every idea starts with a thought that is then grown with imagination. What ideas do you want to grow?

_____

_____

_____

_____

_____

_____

_____

_____

_____

_____

_____

Have you ever noticed that your wildest dreams didn't contain doubts until you spoke about them or laid them all out? Why did you let the doubt in? What is it really about? How do the doubts serve you?

Emotions are not meant to be burdens,
but information. What information
are you receiving regularly?

Are you willing to show up
for yourself?

We've all been given the chance to live on this planet. What will you accomplish with this chance?

_____

_____

_____

_____

_____

_____

_____

_____

_____

_____

If you reflect honestly,
who is dimming your light?

Are you taking responsibility
for yourself and your life?

Growth comes from discomfort—
what is uncomfortable for you right now?

87

Are you allowing space for the good to show
in your life? If so, where do you see it?
If not, what is the benefit of blocking it?

Every time you choose for yourself,
you are the light for other people. You are showing
them that a different choice is possible for them.
What are you choosing for yourself?

What are your first thoughts in the morning?
Do these thoughts make you smile or frown?

(Look at this for at least a week, as it will say a lot about your internal feelings/self.)

What events/experiences/plans do you most look forward to?

Who is responsible for the love
you give yourself?

Author Abraham Hicks said,
"Doubt is your own contraindication of your own
vibration." What doubt do you experience
the most and how has it been limiting you?

What you focus on, you give energy to.
Which things should you stop giving your energy to?

Where do you truly want to focus?
What do you feel is getting in your way?

You can't have an open mind with rigid beliefs.
What beliefs do you hold about yourself?

What beliefs do you hold about others?

What beliefs do you hold about life?

You hold on to your greatest potential
and your biggest disappointment.
Which of the two have you been implementing?

What actions do you take that feed into your greatest potential and your biggest disappointment?

Is your body reacting to your mind? Take note of your thoughts and how you speak. Say something positive and see how your physical body reacts to the words. Now say something negative and see how the body reacts. What did you notice? Again, is your body reacting to your mind in how it feels?

Your mind represents your internal environment
and image of self. How does it look?

The more effort you put in doesn't always equate to better results for your desired outcome. What is your effort level? Is it currently working for you? Do you feel you need to take a step back or increase it?

You are what you believe.
What are you still believing about yourself?

The feeling of being lost is usually a sign
of you becoming more aware.
Where have you been feeling lost lately?

Think of the choices you had/have to make today. Did/do the choices you make feel light? Heavy? A feeling of heaviness is your body's way of telling you not to do/feel something. Try saying, "I am a finite being." You will feel your body contract / become heavy. A feeling of lightness, however, comes from expressing something that is aligned and feels good. Try saying, "I am an infinite being" and feel your body expand / become light.

You are only completely human when you
are playing. What does playing look like for you?

When was the last time you prioritized play?
Do you find play hard to schedule?

Are you constantly chasing happiness / a feeling?
If so, what do you think will happen if you "catch" it?

All judgments can be seen as expressions
of unmet needs. What are the biggest judgments
you are making? What needs do they represent?

The moment you judge yourself,
you lose all ability to influence and impact your life.
What judgment(s) are you putting on yourself?

Conflicting beliefs live in the gap
between your actions and thoughts.
What do you experience conflicting beliefs about?
Where are your actions and values unaligned?

What type of situations/information do you normally avoid?

(This is also where cognitive dissonance lives.)

If you could speak about anything in the present tense as if it is currently happening to you, for you, etc., what would you speak about?

You can make something familiar by telling
your mind/body it is. What would you like to tell
your mind/body? What feeling/emotion would you
pick to be familiar? Continually tell your mind/body
this, especially while in a relaxed state.
What difference do you feel?

You create your beliefs and then they create you.
What creation have you been working
on for the last several years?

Words are powerful, as they form your reality.
What words are you constantly saying?

Are you using your words appropriately
with yourself? With others?
What words do you need to start changing?

What about yourself makes you proud?
Go into detail and state why.

What are two of your toughest memories as a child?
What did you feel in those memories? *(i.e., unworthy,
unloved, etc.)* Do you see these feelings playing out
in current situations at work, home, etc.?

What major life events *(good and bad)*
happened to you or around you from ages 0–5?

What major life events *(good and bad)* happened to you or around you from ages 6–10?

What major life events *(good and bad)*
happened to you or around you from ages 11–15?

What major life events *(good and bad)* happened to you or around you from ages 16–20?

What major life events *(good and bad)*
happened to you or around you from ages 21–25?

What major life events *(good and bad)* happened to you or around you from ages 26–30?

What major life events *(good and bad)*
happened to you or around you from ages 31–35?

What major life events *(good and bad)* happened to you or around you from ages 36–40?

128

What major life events *(good and bad)*
happened to you or around you from ages 41–45?
(Continue to your current age.)

Look over your list of past events.
What do you feel when you look at the list?
What comes up for you?

What connections can you make between how you react today to the past situations in your list? What about yourself makes you proud?

What were some of your defining
or aha moments in life?

Listen. Listen to yourself and others. Listen to the wants, needs, and desires. What is it that you "hear" without your ears? Be sure to listen with your essence for the truth. What do you notice?

The physical body feeds on food, the emotional body feeds on emotions, and the mental body feeds on thoughts and ideas. How would you like to feed yourself today / every day?

Are your choices each day dream-affirmative?
Reflect on your choices in a day
and see where you stand.

Life is a game of love. If you're not loving,
you're not living. What are you loving in life?
What things are you not loving?

Connection holds our greatest potential.
So, what are you connecting to?

We often give the benefit of the doubt to someone's potential, whether it be in friendship, work, or personal relationships. Whose potential have you been waiting on? How has waiting hindered you?

It just takes one step to change your outcome.
What's the one step you need to take?

What's stopping you from taking that step?
When thinking of that step,
what emotions/thoughts/feelings arise?

What feelings have you been pushing down?
Author Karol K. Truman says,
"Feelings buried alive never die."

What is the biggest emotion you feel attached to?
Is it serving you? If not, which emotion
could be serving you better?

What progress have you made in this life,
internally and externally?

What do you most pay attention to with others?
List all positive and negative aspects.

With the list from yesterday, take note of the
negative things you notice. The negative things are
usually a part of your own wounds. What did you
notice and how does that relate to you?

What is unconditional love to you?
How do you experience it?

We can't forget about ourselves when giving and receiving unconditional love. How do you show yourself unconditional love? Do you give yourself unconditional love daily? If you have not started to, how will you moving forward?

Are you viewing the world through a lens of "unconditional love" or through your own "conditions"?
What conditions are you putting on the world?

Our bodies are the most powerful instruments
in the universe. How are you using yours?

What does connection mean to you?
How do you get/feel connection?

What do you feel you do well? What is your
superpower? Ask three people close to you
what they believe your superpower to be.

If you want a true reflection, look at your mother and father and create a list of the things that annoy you about them. Then reflect on your past relationships to see why they didn't work out / current relationships to see where you have the most conflict.
Are you seeing those annoyances in yourself?
Your past and present relationships?
With this awareness, how does that change things?

What is on your must-have list?

(What do you want to give yourself or obtain personally, professionally, and spiritually?)

What is on your
must-NOT-have list?

What unresolved emotions *(memories with charges)*
do you still hold?

What would have to happen
for you to feel grateful?

What fear
is your intellect covering up?

What is true for one person is not always true for another. What are you feeling that is true to you?

When we are not ready to see ourselves,
we will project our biases on others to avoid engaging
in our own needs. What needs are you avoiding?

What relationships in your life are purely
transactional? Why? Would you change
anything about them?

What relationships in your life are purely
transformative? Why? Would you change
anything about them?

_____

_____

_____

_____

_____

_____

_____

_____

_____

_____

_____

The difference between "I have to" and "I choose to"
is the difference between confinement and freedom.
What do you feel or think you have to do?
And what do you feel or think you choose to do?

What does your ideal day look like at this point in your life?

What is stopping you from having that ideal day regularly? What have you done to try and solve it?

_____

_____

_____

_____

_____

_____

_____

_____

_____

_____

We all have a story we tell ourselves that limits us /
isn't congruent with our reality. What's yours?

Do you remember your inner child?
The curiosity that radiated through you?
Where did it go? What dimmed its light?

Are you mindful of your feelings?
Truly mindful of them? Are you able to label them
and take the time to understand them?

What voids have you been trying to fill lately?

If you could release one emotion and/or thought
process, what would it be and why?
What would it do for you? How would you feel?

Behaviors are addictive.
Reflect on which ones you are addicted to that
influence you the most and in the worst way.

Reflect on situations that cause you pain and put into play "consideration." How does that change how you feel? For example, someone at work gets angry at you and lashes out; however, you find out that they have a loved one who is extremely ill. Will you still take on that pain? Or will you be able to understand that it has nothing to do with you?

What are one or two common thoughts
you seem to have ALL the time? What are those
thoughts about? Now, look at them with gratitude
and see how your internal energy shifts.

What resistance
do you have with yourself?

Have you been observing situations
or projecting on situations lately?

How would your life change if just for today
you believed you were enough?

If you knew that a week of neglecting yourself and your emotions would cause a year of needed repair, would you do it? Why or why not?

What areas of yourself
have you been neglecting?

What are you willing to do to make yourself better?
What aren't you willing to do?

What is your willingness to change?
What makes you willing?

What is your one love?
What do you love enough to undergo change?

What do you fear the most?
What is it about that thing that makes you fear it?
What does it bring up?

What would it look like
to be yourself?

What do you feel
defines you?

Where are you right now, mentally, emotionally, and physically? Are you in the present, or are you waiting for and thinking of the next moment/adventure because you think it will be better? If you think it will be better, how so?

Your "yes" has no value until you learn to say "no."
What have you been saying yes to
that you don't want to? What part of you
have you been disrespecting for saying yes?

What are you
yearning for?

Crisis is known to happen when we are playing too small. Where do you see crisis unfolding?

Try starting each day with expansion by saying,
"What else is possible?" How do you think
that will make you feel? What types of
opportunities do you think you will attract?

Thoughts create reality.
What is your current reality?

Who do you feel
you are meant to be?

What inspires you?

Are you still blaming yourself/others
instead of looking for a better option?
Who are you blaming and for what?
What is a better use of energy?

Life never compromises itself. Life is for us.
How are you compromising life/yourself?

What did you learn in the past year that you love?
A passion? A personal trait?
It can be anything new to you.

What makes you unique? How do you harness it?
If you don't know, ask five people around you
what stands out about you to them.
Then think of things you are also extremely good at.

When you look at yourself and others,
do you see the whole person? Do you see the whole
tree? Can you see the roots that are beneath the
ground? Look at yourself. What part do people see
(trunk/limbs/leaves)? What part don't people see *(soil, roots)*?

How are you analyzing yourself? If you aren't yet, analyze yourself now. What do you notice?

If you weren't burdened with worry,
how would you live your life?

If you knew you were going to get to your
end goal no matter what, would you still
be worried about the "how"? What is it about
the how that is holding you back?

What would happen if you looked at your
stressors as learnings/opportunities to grow?

Reflect on your hardest times in life.
What beauty came from them?

Reflect on the three people who hurt you the most.
What lessons came from it?

Where does your good come from? (You'll have to define what *good* is to you to answer this question.)

When you're feeling stuck/hurt, what is your go-to?
What is your vice? Does it actually help?
Or is it just instant gratification?

You can't wake up someone
who is pretending to sleep. Are you pretending
to sleep anywhere in your life?

Where might you be trying to wake someone
pretending to sleep?
Is it your responsibility to wake them?

Nothing really has power unless you give power to it.
What are you giving power to that isn't serving you?

What would be in your highest
and best interest to give power to?

If it were your last week on earth,
how would you spend it?

(Take note of the things you state and implement them more in your everyday life. These are the things that are most important to you.)

Emotions are like children—they just want
to be acknowledged and heard. What emotions
are trying to be heard/acknowledged?

Your passion/purpose evolves from around
the ages of 7–14. What did you love to do
between those ages?

Reflect and think about when you felt self-doubt. Now, think of memories that solidified that you should have self-doubt. Are they even there? If so, and if you observe those memories from a third-person perspective, what do you notice?

Expectations lead to disappointment if the results are different than planned. What expectations are you holding on to for yourself? For others? For life?

What does forgiveness
mean to you?

Have you
fully forgiven yourself?

When you think of others that have hurt you,
have you fully forgiven them,
or do you still hold pain inside?

_____

_____

_____

_____

_____

_____

_____

_____

_____

_____

It's not what you look at but rather what you see.
What are you seeing within your life?

We are all individual parts made into a whole. However, we sometimes try to disown/ignore certain parts within us. What parts of you are you trying to avoid/disown?

Do you feel whole? If you answered no, what parts of you aren't who you are meant to be? What is the vital component that would help you feel whole? If you answered yes, how would you describe that wholeness? What is the vital component that helps you feel whole?

What aspects of you have you dimmed
in order to seem bright to others?

(Think in regard to parents, friends, coworkers, your boss, etc.)

What are you hungry for?
What do you crave mentally, physically, and socially?

If you numb pain, you lose the ability to experience all positives in life. Which would you rather do? What pain don't you want to feel? What positives in life have the biggest impact on you?

_____

_____

_____

_____

_____

_____

_____

_____

_____

_____

What current motivator gets you out of bed in the morning?

Is all of you showing up to life
or just the parts that you deem necessary?

What parts do you deem necessary?
What parts aren't showing up?

You can't run away from your past. Instead,
shine a light on it. Reflect. What do you feel?
Sit with it and feel the effect in your body.
Where do you feel it? Now, observe and feel
its presence for a while. Does it change?

Look back on your life. What can you see
that helps/allows you to move forward?

Identity is never set in stone. What would you say
your identity is now and where do you want it to go?

What does commitment look like to you?

Are you committed to yourself?
How are you showing yourself that you are?

When you look and feel into your heart,
what do you notice about yourself?

Author Toni Morrison said,
"Definitions belong to the definers, not the defined."
Are you taking on the definition of the definers?
How do you define yourself?

We create our experience in this world.
What experience are you creating?

_____

_____

_____

_____

_____

_____

_____

_____

_____

_____

_____

233

Life is all about belief systems—good and bad. Usually, we create a belief that serves us in some way; however, we can and do outgrow certain beliefs. When this happens and we don't alter our beliefs in ways that align with us, they become negative. What belief systems do you hold that were once positive but are now negative?

In your own destruction, you carry
your own medicine—are you willing to see it?
Do you truly want to see it?
What will change if you were to see/use it?

One of the most revealing things in life is chaos.
Reflect on the chaos you've observed in life.
What do you see?

What do you truly fear about
your own emotions / the depth of yourself?

Things are not what they are, they are how you are.
So, in looking back at situations, how were you then?

If you were to listen to what was really being said versus the words being used, how do you think your relationships would change?

_____

_____

_____

_____

_____

_____

_____

_____

_____

_____

_____

Everything we know now was once considered unknown to us. So, at what point did you become afraid of following through with the unknown?

Connection is the key to life.
How do you connect with yourself?
With others? With life?

Our experience of life is both subjective
and objective in the same proportion.
How does that knowledge alter the way you
see others and how they are living their life?

Every person who enters your life contributes to your growth either by showing you what's not going to be conducive to it or what will be conducive. Reflect on your past friendships/relationships. What did they teach you that was favorable to your growth? What did they teach you that you don't want to implement?

Think of the memory that causes you the most pain. What if you could see it as a whole picture instead of just through the lens of emotion? What learnings can you take away from it? Picture it as an observer.

We are creative beings. To not create is to suppress your true self. What creative outlets are you drawn to do? If you don't do them, why not?

Many people seem to dread their emotions
and psyche. However, our emotions and psyche
allow us to live. What is your most "alive" memory?
What has made you feel like you were living?

If that feeling made you feel alive,
how can you bring that more into your life?

_____

_____

_____

_____

_____

_____

_____

_____

_____

_____

When we don't understand something,
we sometimes deem it meaningless or worthless.
What about yourself have you deemed meaningless
or worthless because you do not understand it?

It is through error that we learn and gather knowledge and wisdom. What have been some of your biggest errors?

Does an artist's work explain the artist or their life outside of their art? All too often we define ourselves by the art we have created, when in reality, it is a reflection of our circumstances, not our whole being. What "art" of yours are you letting define/explain you?

To grasp life's meaning, we must let our experiences shape us. Experiences, whether we like them or not, have shaped others before us and will continue to shape others after us. Which life experiences have truly shaped you?

Many people believe that we are the contents of our minds; however, we are far more than that. If you could empty out the "not so great" contents of your mind, what would you have left?

Do we learn more from our failures or from our successes? Consider failures as stepping stones that allow us to put forth another stone to step forward. Now, look at where you may still feel like a failure. What stepping stones have you started to create?

Actions speak louder than words, but unconscious actions speak the loudest. What unconscious actions do you see in your loved ones that hurt you?

(You can always ask those closest to you for some insight in addition to reflecting on your own.)

Psychologist George Loewenstein stated that curiosity is "a cognitive induced deprivation that arises from the perception of a gap in knowledge and understanding."

Where are you "deprived" in your perception of yourself and what areas can be exposed in the most beautiful way? A way that allows you to dig deeper into yourself and see who you truly are?

How much of your happiness is dependent
on others? If we take it a step further,
why do you feel that it is?

Are you truly treating yourself well? *(Not just with your thoughts, but with movement, nutrition, and connection?)*

What area of your life is most neglected?

Movement is our body's natural expression.
Are you truly allowing expression?

The whole point of self-development is not simply to learn and reiterate but to experience, reflect, and apply the new learnings and awareness to our everyday life.

How have you applied your life learnings / personal development thus far?

We live on three planes of understanding:
we are spiritual, we have an intellect,
and we live in physical bodies. What planes of
understanding have you not been present with?

When we lack an understanding of who
we are it means we are reacting to life instead
of living. Where have you just been reacting?
What aspects of you have just been reacting to life?

What part of you do you feel
you don't truly understand?

If you didn't rush to get things done, how would your relationship with yourself and others change?

The body believes what your mind tells it.
How have you been speaking to yourself?
What are the main things you say about yourself?
Are they positive or negative?

What makes you
feel heard?

Sometimes what makes you uncomfortable is actually good for you. What makes you uncomfortable?

People sometimes rely on a crutch
for their circumstances *(i.e., I have ADHD
so I can't do that)*. Is there a crutch you rely on?

How many things do you feel you should do but
don't? What is the emotion behind the should?
What do you feel it provides for you?

_____

_____

_____

_____

_____

_____

_____

_____

_____

_____

If you kept living the life you are currently living,
would you be happy with it?

What are you feeling/needing/wanting in conversations with your work relationships? Friend relationships? Family relationships? Are you talking to get validation, to feel more worthy, to be right, to discuss?

(Reflect each time you start a conversation to see the true purpose behind it.)

If you were to look at all the projects in life you've done, did you get more accomplished out of fear or love? Which is your driving force?

If you are doing something out of fear,
how would it change if you did it out of love?

No person or thing can hold your mind captive
unless you allow them/it to.
Who/What usually holds your mind captive?

Things are not always what they are,
they are how you are. How are you right now?

274

What lenses have you been seeing the world through in the last while? Has that been making you feel positive or negative? If negative, are you willing to change your lenses?

What benefit(s) have you incurred from seeing through those lenses? What disadvantages have you had?

Awareness is a prerequisite for change.
How do you know when you become aware?

What do you want from
your friendships?

What do you want from your romantic relationship?

What do you feel is lacking
in your relationship with yourself and others?

What part of yourself
are you not intimate with?

What areas in your life
do you need to integrate better?

How often do you prioritize others' needs over your own? What situations do you do that in most often?

Without placing value on things, you cannot generate meaning. What value have you not placed on things in your life?

_____

_____

_____

_____

_____

_____

_____

_____

_____

_____

The source of our wholeness is unowned
and reality lives through us. Reality is a story.
So what story are you telling yourself?

Everything that you see happening to you
is but a mere perception.
What are you seeing happening to you?

Momentum can go in any direction.
Which way has your momentum taken you lately?
Are you happy with it? If not, are you willing
to see momentum move in a different direction?
Yes? How will you do that for yourself?

What distractions do you incur that make you feel more contracted?

(This can be from strangers, coworkers, partners, siblings, friends, etc.)

It's quite easy to get sedentary in life.
What areas of your life are getting sedentary?

Your expectations create your reality.
What are you expecting from yourself
and how is that affecting you?

The expectations you have for yourself—are they actually yours? Which ones are and aren't?

The philosopher Osho said, "You will come closer and closer to perfection, but you will never be perfect. Perfection is not the way of existence. Growth is the way." Where in your life have you been trying to be perfect? What do you feel will happen once you accomplish "perfection"?

What are your healthy/dream-affirmative and
unhealthy/dream-diminishing manifestations?

How do you identify yourself? Is it through external or internal sources? When you reflect on that identity, do you relate to it?

What is the one service you feel
moved to give to the world?

Everyone has a secret story that isn't true that
they tell themselves. It robs them of their unique
self. It's the one thing that hinders them.
What is the secret story you tell yourself?

Truthfully, we are never lost, as we are always home.
Holistic lifestyle coach Paul Chek said, "Non-locality
is the nature of the soul." If you're feeling lost,
you're usually going against your sense of self.
Where have you been going against your sense of self?

What is pulling you away from your sense of self?
Is it a person? A belief system? An experience?

_____

_____

_____

_____

_____

_____

_____

_____

_____

_____

Asking questions / reflecting on yourself
is the difference between doing and being.
Are you asking yourself to grow?

Who do you admire and look up to?
Why?

Fear is a good indication for what we will or need to deal with next. What fear do you have that you need to deal with next?

How do you handle stress? Do you need to be by yourself? Do you need to be social? Do you lean more toward food? Do you tend to eat less? Do different types of stress affect you differently?

(i.e., work stress versus financial stress versus life stress)

Whose input
do you value most?

Whose opinion influences you the most?
Reflect on how they make you feel
and on the deep roots of why that may be.

From the last two questions, are they the same people or are they different? Why do you feel that is?

How do you
feel validated?

Whose validation
do you seek most often/most?

When were the last three times
you challenged yourself in a beautiful way? How?

How do you plan on challenging
yourself moving forward?

What does balance in life look like to you?

How do you know when
you have achieved balance?

What makes you feel recharged/rejuvenated?

How much stress do you put on external possession versus essentials? In other words, if we were to look at all your stressors, are they "false" possession stressors or essential-life stressors like water, food, and shelter?

Carl Jung stated, "Everything that irritates us about others can lead us to a better understanding of ourselves." What irritates you the most? Where does this irritation/memory stem from? What is the true underlying cause of it?

What is one theme that has been constantly present in your life? Are you willing to stop resisting it?

Esther Veltheim stated, "There is only one reason you experience inner conflict. Someone *(or something)* is living at the center of your life." What is currently living at the center of your life?

How do you handle conflict? Do you project?
Do you shut down? Do you need time to process it?
How does it change in/with different settings/topics?
With friends, coworkers, parents,
partners, siblings, children, etc.?

What does responsibility
mean and look like to you?

How much responsibility
do you really want to take/have in life?

How does the amount of responsibility
change between work, life, etc.?

When you reflect on where you are now in your life, what is your initial thought? Did you instantly go to a negative thought or a positive one?

What unites us as individuals is far greater
than our differences. What differences have you
let get in the way of uniting with others?

What polar opinion do you hold?
(Polar opinions are the extreme opposites of the ones other people hold.) What would be the middle ground?

All polarization limits our view.
What polarizations do you have that have been
limiting your view of the world/others?

Is there a difference between how you show up
with others versus how you show up for yourself?

What are five traits/characteristics you truly value and appreciate about yourself?

What does intimacy
mean to you?

How do you create intimacy with yourself?
With others? With nature/With the world?

When you reflect/observe, do you generate your thoughts based on rational/objective facts? Or are you guided more by irrational/subjective aspects?

What would happen if you paid attention to both the objective and subjective and allowed them to dance together? How would your life/world change?

The day you say you know someone is the day you stop paying attention to them. Whom do you think you know that you've stopped paying attention to?

There is no desire without devotion.
What have you been devoting yourself to?
What desire are you trying to obtain?

Being unable to communicate the hardest things in life often leads to loneliness. What have you been having a hard time communicating?

333

What emotion*(s)* do you have the hardest time
connecting to and communicating?

334

Based on the last question, what is the first
memory you have of experiencing that emotion?
What was going on that made it difficult
to connect and/or communicate?

How have you been using your mind the majority of the time? Is it your servant or your master?

True mastery of spirit and self is taking a negative
and seeing it as positive / turning it into a positive.
What are ten things that were once negative
that you can now consider positive?

Through the course of the day/week,
think every time before you make a decision.
Are your choices and actions creating harmony
or disharmony within yourself?

If everyone around the world
made the same choices and actions you are,
would the world be a better place?

How long are you able to be by yourself?
How long can you be in silence?

There is no ego in silence. When was the last time you listened for the answers you seek? If you're currently looking for an answer to a problem, sit in silence and write down the answer that comes.

You are rarely upset for the reason you think. Usually, it is an underlying fear-based response that reminds you of a past experience. Take a look at what has upset you over the last week.
Can you recall similar situations in the past?

If you extended love to whoever upset you,
whether it be others or yourself,
how would that change the circumstance?

If you realized that you personally choose
the feelings you want to experience regardless
of others actions/words toward you
(in other words, you can be responsible for what you see/feel),
how would that change your life on a daily basis?

What emotions continuously come up for you?
The emotions you seem to always recycle through?

Think back to when your younger self was
struggling the most. What would you tell them?

You are responsible for owning your role
in every situation; thus, blame is not actually true.
It is but an egoic response. If you reflect
on situations where you placed blame,
what responsibility would you take on now?

The essence of living in spirit is a sense of
self-awareness. What areas of self-awareness
do you feel you need to explore more?

Who do you think GOD is? *(Note: This question is not based on any religion. GOD can be whichever higher power you choose.)*

Are there limitations to your thoughts?
Do you shut down when I use the word GOD?
Does GOD provide you with pain or comfort?

When I say the word neighbor, what does
that mean to you? Who and what are neighbors
to you and how do you look to treat them?

_____

_____

_____

_____

_____

_____

_____

_____

_____

_____

What makes
your heart sing?

How do you listen to your heart?
How do you know when it's your heart
guiding you versus your head or ego?

Where in your life are you constantly
feeling conflicted? How long has it been that way?
Are you putting up with it just out of comfort?

To make a decision is not a matter of choosing between equal alternatives, it's making an enlightened choice in regard to our inner self—it's the difference between an "ego" decision and a "self" decision. In recalling the decisions of your past, were they "ego" driven or "self" driven? In taking this into consideration, how will this change your decisions moving forward?

What masks do you put on in different situations?
Why? For whom?

What do you deem right? And what do you deem wrong? How do you know that something is right or wrong? Things that you deem wrong, are they actually wrong? Or do they just not make sense to you? And if they just don't make sense to you, are they still wrong if they make sense to someone else?

The judgments you have about others/yourself,
are they really true?

357

Do the judgments you hold bring you
a greater connection to life?
Do they create a greater connection to the
people you want to be surrounded by?

How do you create ever greater wholeness
for yourself? For others?

The love you have for the people in your life—
how would you describe that love?

(Reflect honestly. Is it from a codependent state?
Or from a whole state?)

Saying no to yourself creates limitations.
What have you been saying no to when you
could be saying yes? What areas of your life
do you want to expand but keep playing small?

The opposite of belief is knowing—knowing
is a personified experience. When you turn knowing
into a noun, it becomes a belief. What have you been
stating you know when it is simply just a belief?
Are you willing to relook at it?

Do the people you spend the most time with
bring you ease or tension?

What is your mission?

364

Let me ask again:
Who are you?

BRITTANY BIRD is currently undergoing her
doctorate and PhD in integrative medicine.
She is a manual osteopath and holds credentials
as a BodyTalk Practitioner and Holistic Lifestyle
Coach. Brittany believes in and utilizes a whole-
body approach in her practice, with her patients
encompassing all levels of being—mental,
emotional, and physical—to help with healing.